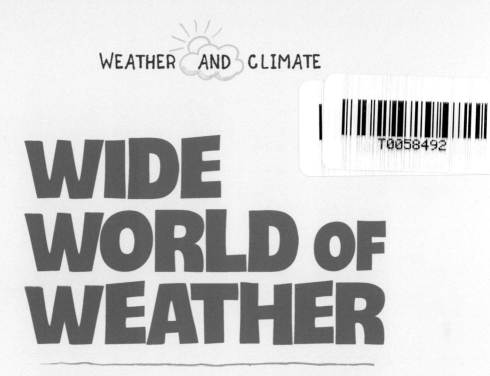

WEATHER AND CLIMATE

WIDE WORLD OF WEATHER

WEATHER AND CLIMATE AROUND THE WORLD

by Emily Raij

CAPSTONE PRESS
a capstone imprint

Capstone Captivate is published by Capstone Press, an imprint of Capstone.
1710 Roe Crest Drive, North Mankato, Minnesota, 56003.
www.capstonepub.com

Library of Congress Cataloging-in-Publication Data is available on the Library of
Congress website.
ISBN: 978-1-5435-9158-3 (library binding)
ISBN: 978-1-4966-5780-0 (paperback)
ISBN: 978-1-5435-9163-7 (ebook pdf)

Summary: Describes weather and climate, the weather experienced in each climate
type, and how climate impacts people, animals, and plant life.

Image Credits
iStockphoto/zhongguo, cover (bottom left); Shutterstock: Adwo, 8, Alessandro
Zappalorto, 21, Alex Lerner, 19, Cre8 design, cover (top left), fokke baarssen, 29,
FootageLab, 20, Gerhard Strydom, cover (bottom right), guentermanaus, 10, I.
Noyan Yilmaz, 25, Jarmo Piironen, 15, jejiim, 13, John D Sirlin, cover (bottom right),
Jon Ingall, 12, juerginho, 27, Kodda, 26, Konstantnin, 18, Maciej Czekajewski, 11,
Mo Wu, 4, Nym3ria, 5, Oleksandr Katrusha, 23, Rawpixel.com, 28, risteski goce, 22,
Sander van der Werf, cover (top right), 1, Soleil Nordic, 7, Tarpan, 9, 16, Troutnut, 17,
vladsilver, 24

Artistic elements: Shutterstock; gigi rosa, MaddyZ, Rebellion Works

Editorial Credits
Editor: Erika L. Shores; Designer: Tracy McCabe; Media Researcher: Kelly Garvin;
Premedia Specialist: Kathy McColley

All internet sites appearing in back matter were available and accurate when this
book was sent to press.

Capstone thanks Rachel Humphrey, assistant professor, Department of Atmospheric
and Hydrologic Sciences, St. Cloud State University, St. Cloud, MN, for her expertise
in reviewing this book.

TABLE OF CONTENTS

Words in **bold** are in the glossary.

CHAPTER 1

WEATHER AND CLIMATE

Whoosh! Wind is howling outside. Snow is falling fast. It's a cold winter night in New York City. No one wants to go outside. Across the world in the country of Australia, it's a different story. The sun is shining. Temperatures are rising. Beaches are full of people. How can the weather be so different on the same planet and at the same time?

People gather on sandy beaches during summer on Australia's coasts.

Weather is what's happening in the **atmosphere** from day to day. Wind and temperature are weather conditions that can change all the time.

Climate is the average weather conditions over a very long period of time. There are many factors affecting climate. The way those factors affect climate is different in each region, or part, of the world. That's why each region has its own climate.

Snow piles up during a blizzard in New York City.

Many things affect the climate of a place. How close an area is to a large body of water is one factor. Ocean and wind **currents**, or movements, also affect climate. The features of the land and the height of land above sea level are two more factors.

One of the biggest effects on a location's climate is its **latitude**. That is an area's distance from the **equator**. The equator is a made-up line that divides Earth into northern and southern halves.

Earth's **axis** is always tilting the same way. This causes the sun to shine more or less on different areas at different times. That is how we get seasons as Earth moves around the sun.

Since Earth's axis is tilted, locations closer to the equator get more direct sunlight throughout the year. These places are called the tropics. They have warmer climates than places farther from the equator.

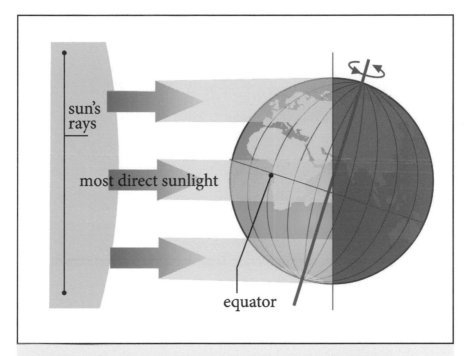

During the day, areas along the equator receive more direct sunlight. This is because the areas are closer to the sun than the northern and southern parts of Earth.

CHAPTER 2

DIFFERENT CLIMATE TYPES

A climate is based on temperature, how much and when **precipitation** happens, and what grows in the area. Main climate types are desert, tropical, temperate, and polar.

DESERT CLIMATE

Desert climates are dry. They get fewer than 10 inches (25 centimeters) of precipitation all year. The air in a desert holds less moisture than in wetter climates. Desert air has less water. There is not enough water to contain the day's heat. That means nights are cold. The big change in temperature from day to night makes it hard to live in desert climates.

FACT

The driest spot outside of Antarctica is the Atacama Desert in northern Chile. A city there went without water for 400 years!

Many deserts get very hot. Some deserts can reach 122 degrees Fahrenheit (50 degrees Celsius). But not all deserts are hot. Antarctica is a desert. It is the coldest place on Earth. But it doesn't rain or snow much. Antarctica has the coldest, windiest, and driest climate in the world.

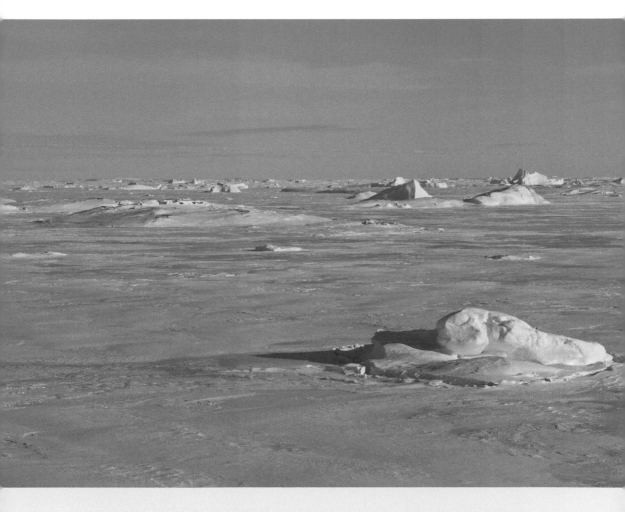

The icy Antarctic desert

TROPICAL CLIMATE

Tropical climates are hot all year. They have average temperatures warmer than 64°F (18°C).

Rain forests are tropical climates with lots of rain. They get 50 to 250 inches (127 to 635 cm) each year. One example is the Amazon rain forest in South America. It is the world's biggest rain forest. More than half of the world's types of plants and animals live in rain forests. Plants grow well in the warm, wet air.

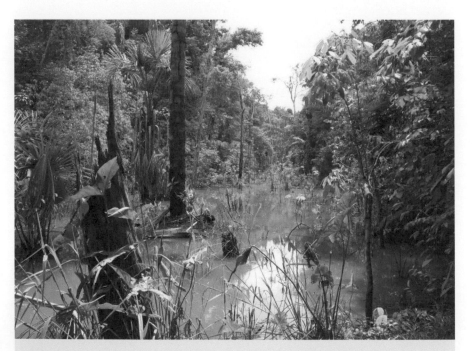

The Amazon rain forest is in Brazil. Brazil is in South America.

Other tropical climates are hot all year but have a wet and dry season. These areas are called **savannas**. Africa has many. Tall grasses grow in savannas. Plants and trees can survive through **droughts** there. North and South America and Australia also have savannas.

A savanna in the African country of Kenya

TEMPERATE CLIMATE

Temperate climates are usually not too hot and not too cold. They have average temperatures warmer than 50°F (10°C). There is also not a lot of rain or snow all year. They get an average of 11 to 79 inches (30 to 200 cm) each year. But daily temperatures and weather can change quite a bit. One day it might be hot and sunny. The next day might bring rain and cold. There are different types of temperate climates.

Plants grow well near the Mediterranean Sea.

One type of temperate climate is affected by ocean or sea winds and currents. Areas near the Mediterranean Sea have warm, dry summers and short, rainy winters. It doesn't get very cold. Western Europe and western North America have this type of climate too. Mild temperatures mean lots of plants can grow here.

California's coast is along the Pacific Ocean. It has a temperate climate.

Continental is a type of temperate climate. Places with continental climates have four seasons. Spring is warm and wet. Summer is hot and fairly dry. Fall is cool and dry. Winters are cold with snow and lots of wind.

The midwestern United States, southern Canada, and central Europe have continental climates. It can rain or snow year-round. There is enough moisture for many trees and plants to grow. Most trees in continental climates lose their leaves in fall and winter.

Another type of temperate climate is **subarctic**. It has long, very cold winters and short, cool summers. Much of Alaska, Canada, Russia, and Iceland is subarctic. Most of these areas have little precipitation.

A HUGE FOREST

The boreal forest has a subarctic climate. It spreads across many countries. These include Canada, Alaska in the United States, Russia, Norway, Sweden, Finland, and even parts of Japan. It makes up one-third of the world's forest area.

The trees of the boreal forest cover much of Finland in northern Europe.

POLAR CLIMATE

The polar climate at the North and South Poles is freezing! The North Pole, or Arctic, is surrounded by the Arctic Ocean with floating sheets of ice. The South Pole is on Antarctica. The land there is covered in thick ice. The average winter temperature in the Arctic is -30° F (-34°C). At the South Pole, it's -76°F (-60°C).

Although snow is rare, it builds up over long periods of time in Antarctica.

The sun shines all day from March through September at the North Pole, and all day from September through March at the South Pole. Most of the Arctic is too cold and dry for trees to grow. But during summer, a thin layer of soil thaws. Grass grows. Yellow poppies bloom too. At the South Pole, some small plants grow in places that are not always covered in snow and ice.

Only small plants are found in the freezing Arctic.

CHAPTER 3

LIFE IN DIFFERENT CLIMATES

DESERT LIFE

Desert plants and animals can live with little water and extreme heat. The cactus stores water in its stem. Other plants and flowers only bloom when it rains. Desert foxes get the liquid they need from eating other animals. To keep cool during the day, many desert animals stay underground or under rocks. They hunt only in the cooler night.

FACT

Camels do well in deserts. Camels have two rows of eyelashes. They also have nostrils that close. Both keep out sand. Fat stored in their humps lets them go days without food and water.

People have ways to survive living in hot deserts. The Bedouin tribe of the Middle East lives in tents. The cloth walls allow air to flow. Tents are lined with animal hair. This keeps heat and cold in or out when needed.

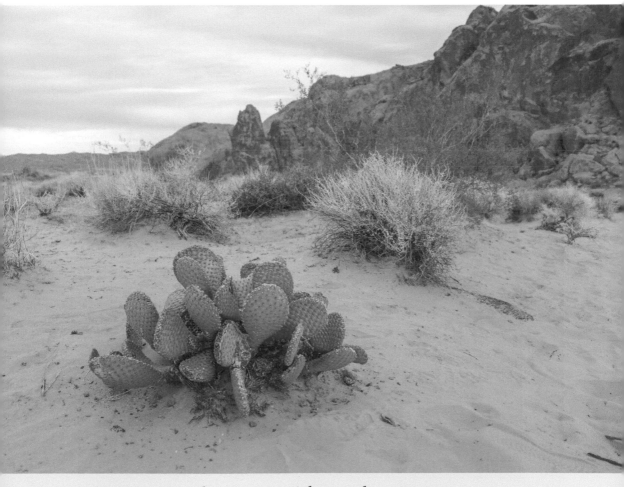

Cacti grow in the deserts of the southwestern United States.

TROPICAL LIFE

Trees in tropical rain forests grow tall. Their branches and leaves stretch out to form a **canopy**, or cover, over the forest. When a dead tree falls, it lets in sunlight. Then a new tree can grow. The canopy is also home to many animals. Colorful birds fill the trees. Monkeys swing from high branches.

A tropical rain forest

Some people live in rain forests. They hunt and fish rain forest animals. They eat fruits and nuts from rain forest plants. Some people grow their own food.

Houses in tropical places are sometimes built on stilts. This keeps water from flooding the homes. Stilts also let breezes flow under the houses to cool them.

A house on stilts in the Amazon rain forest

TEMPERATE LIFE

Plants in temperate climates must survive dry summers. Pine, cypress, and oak trees are found here. Olive, fig, grape, and citrus trees also grow well. There are small shrubs and herbs but not large patches of grass. That means animals, such as goats, sheep, and rabbits, can't eat only grass. They must eat other plants.

In continental forests, trees change with the seasons. Trees lose their leaves when temperatures turn cold in fall and winter. They grow again in warm spring weather.

Olive trees grow in temperate climates.

Many animals are suited for life in climates with changing seasons. Black bears have thick fur to stay warm during winter. They go into dens and sleep when it gets very cold. They live off their body fat. Squirrels store food and nest in trees during winter.

Red squirrels live in trees during winter in temperate climates.

POLAR LIFE

Animals such as penguins, seals, and fish call Antarctica home. Penguins and seals have a thick layer of fat to stay warm. The blood of some fish is special so they can stay alive in icy waters.

At the North Pole, polar bears are at home. They blend in with the snow. This helps polar bears sneak up on and catch other animals to eat.

Penguins dive into the water to hunt for fish.

In Antarctica, at any given time, there are about 75 camps where scientists live and work. As many as 1,000 scientists are there in the winter months. In summer, 4,000 scientists work there. There are also spots that tourists visit in Antarctica.

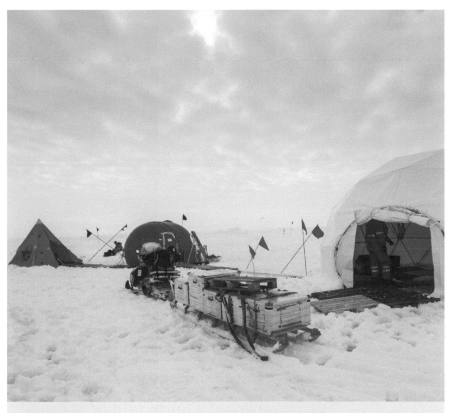

A small camp made by scientists near the South Pole

CHAPTER 4

HOW IS CLIMATE CHANGING?

Changes in the world's climate are making it harder for plants and animals to survive. People are the biggest cause of this change. Burning **fossil fuels** such as coal, oil, and natural gas releases **carbon dioxide** into the air. Fossil fuels are used to power cars and make electricity. Carbon dioxide absorbs heat. Heat gets trapped by Earth's atmosphere and creates warmer temperatures.

A power plant burns coal to make energy. Burning coal adds carbon dioxide to the air.

Hotter temperatures hurt the places where animals live and the food they eat. Sometimes animals move to new areas. But they don't always do well in their new homes.

Hotter temperatures can cause corn and other crops to die in fields.

A SPREADING DESERT

Rising temperatures are causing dry areas to spread. The Sahara is in Africa. It is the largest warm-weather desert. It has grown 10 percent since 1920. More heat and less rainfall make it harder to grow food.

Climate change affects every type of climate. Seasons and life cycles have shifted. Precipitation patterns have changed. Some places get bigger storms. Warmer temperatures mean spring comes earlier in some places. Migrating animals may return before there is food available to eat. In some places there is less water and less good land to grow food. Plants and animals are losing their homes.

Recycling plastic means less resources will be used to make new plastic.

LOOKING TO THE FUTURE

Most countries are working to lower how much carbon dioxide they put into the air. Businesses are using more clean energy. This includes energy from the wind and sun. Using energy made by the wind and the sun does not add carbon dioxide to the atmosphere. Many people are also lowering their carbon dioxide **pollution**. Some are driving electric cars instead of cars that burn gas. They are recycling and reusing everyday items. We can all help protect the climates around the world.

Energy created by wind turbines does not add carbon dioxide to the air.

GLOSSARY

atmosphere (AT-muhss-fihr)—the mixture of gases that surrounds Earth

axis (AK-sis)—a real or imaginary line through the center of an object, around which the object turns

canopy (KA-nuh-pee)—the middle layer of the rain forest where the greenery is thick and there is little sunlight

carbon dioxide (KAHR-buhn dy-AHK-syd)—a gas that has no smell or color

climate (KLY-muht)—the average weather in a place over many years

current (KUHR-uhnt)—the movement of air or of water in a river or an ocean

drought (DROUT)—a long period of weather with little or no rainfall

equator (i-KWAY-tuhr)—an imaginary line around the middle of Earth; it divides the northern and southern hemispheres

fossil fuel (FAH-suhl FYOOL)—natural fuel formed from the remains of plants and animals; coal, oil, and natural gas are fossil fuels

latitude (LAT-i-tood)—the distance measured north or south of the equator

pollution (puh-LOO-shuhn)—substances that make air, land, and water dirty and not safe to use

precipitation (pri-sip-i-TAY-shuhn)—water that falls from the clouds in the form of rain, hail, or snow

savanna (suh-VAN-uh)—a flat, grassy area of land with few or no trees

subarctic (sub-ARK-tik)—areas directly south of the Arctic Circle; the Arctic Circle is an imaginary line just south of the North Pole

READ MORE

Machajewski, Sarah. *Weather and Climate Around the World.* New York: PowerKids Press, 2018.

Maloof, Torrey. *Climate.* Huntington Beach, CA: Teacher Created Materials, Inc., 2015.

Senker, Cath. *Temperate Climates.* Chicago: Capstone, 2017.

INTERNET SITES

Marina Ventura's Climate Explorers
https://www.funkidslive.com/learn/marina-ventura/climate-explorers/major-climate-zones-world/#

NASA Climate Kids
https://climatekids.nasa.gov/weather-climate/

INDEX